DIY Slim

30 Recipes For Colorful Variety Of Stress Relieving Slimes

Copyright 2016 by publisher - All rights reserved.

This document is geared towards providing exact and reliable information in regards to the topic and issue covered. The publication is sold with the idea that the publisher is not required to render accounting, officially permitted, or otherwise, qualified services. If advice is necessary, legal or professional, a practiced individual in the profession should be ordered.

- From a Declaration of Principles which was accepted and approved equally by a Committee of the American Bar Association and a Committee of Publishers and Associations.

In no way is it legal to reproduce, duplicate, or transmit any part of this document in either electronic means or in printed format. Recording of this publication is strictly prohibited and any storage of this document is not allowed unless with written permission from the publisher. All rights reserved.

The information provided herein is stated to be truthful and consistent, in that any liability, in terms of inattention or otherwise, by any usage or abuse of any policies, processes, or directions contained within is the solitary and utter responsibility of the recipient reader. Under no circumstances will any legal responsibility or blame be held against the publisher for any reparation, damages, or monetary loss due to the information herein, either directly or indirectly.

Respective authors own all copyrights not held by the publisher.

The information herein is offered for informational purposes solely, and is universal as so. The presentation of the information is without contract or any type of guarantee assurance.

The trademarks that are used are without any consent, and the publication of the trademark is without permission or backing by the trademark owner. All trademarks and brands within this book are for clarifying purposes only and are the owned by the owners themselves, not affiliated with this document.

Table of content

Introduction 6
Chapter 1 – 20 Simple Stress Relieving Slime Recipes 9
1. The Basic Slime Ball 9
2. Glue Ball 11
3. Glitter Slime 12
4. Lavender Putty 13
5. Scented Goo 15
6. The Squidgy Slime Ball 17
7. Slime Without Liquid starch (Shampoo) 18
8. Volcano Fluffy Slime 20
9. Sand Slime 21
10. Magnetic Slime 22
11. Saline Slime 23
12. Crunchy Slime 25
13. Floam Slime 26
14. Super Stretchy Slime 27
15. Putty Slime 28
16. Edible Slime! 30
17. Soap Slime 31
18. Two Ingredient Slime 32
19. No Glue Slime – Chia Seed 33
20. Seedless No Glue Slime 34

Chapter 2 – 10 Fun Variations OF Slime Recipes 36
   1.   No Borax Slime 36
   2.   Liquid Soap Glitter Slime 37
   3.   Yoghurt Slime! 38
   4.   Borax & Glue Free Slime 39
   5.   Rainbow Slime 40
   6.   Heated Slime 41
   7.   Glow in the Dark 42
   8.   Confetti Slime 43
   9.   Bubbling Slime 44
   10.   The Most Basic Slime 45

Conclusion 47

Introduction

Stress is something that everyone lives with and yet it remains one of the biggest killers. It is often referred to as 'the silent killer'. This is because elevated levels of stress have been linked with heart disease, irregular heartbeats and a variety of other heart issues.

But stress is also an essential part of the human make-up. Whenever you find yourself in a stressful situation your body releases a hormone called cortisol. This prepares your brain and muscles so that you are ready to fight or run. It is one of the most primitive responses of modern man but a natural self-preservation system.

The real issue isn't that you get stressed is that your body doesn't know the difference between a life and death mugging and a stressful meeting with your boss. In the modern, hectic world this means that your body spends much of its time ready to fight or flight.

Unfortunately, the release of cortisol into your system inhibits many of your normal everyday functions and places huge amounts of pressure on your vital organs; specifically your heart.

There are many ways to lower your stress levels, change jobs, laugh or simply remove yourself from the situation. However, not all of these are practical options. Laughing in the middle of an important but stressful meeting with your boss will not help your overall situation!

This is why you need a stress reliever on hand, on to be exact, in hand. Stress relieving slime does exactly that. The act of squeezing it in your hand is enough to detract you from the stress of the situation; this allows your cortisol levels to drop reducing the stress on your body and the long term health implications.

Slime is a great way of reducing stress and the best part of it is that you can make lots of different versions of it at home for very little money. This means that you can have an array of different stress relieving limes according to the situation or mood you find yourself in. The great thing about this is that you don't need to get stressed if you lose one of your slime balls, you should have others and you can easily make more.

Slime balls can also be good as a distraction. For instance, if you are always biting your nails, even though you know it's not a good habit, you can use a slime ball to keep your hands busy, preventing the ability to bite your nails.

The idea behind the stress relieving slime ball is that your slime is always on hand to calm your mind. The simple act of squeezing and pulling the slime allows you to evaluate the issue in hand and calmly move on. It might not prevent you getting stressed but it can prevent you from staying stressed. By avoiding high levels of stress you will reduce your chances of heart disease, strokes and even cancer. All of this is possible through the use of the humble stress relieving slime ball!

It's time to start learning how to make some!

Chapter 1 – 20 Simple Stress Relieving Slime Recipes

The beauty of slime is that it is easy to make and generally only requires ingredients you already have at home. Each of the following 15 recipes is very simple to make:

1. **The Basic Slime Ball**

This is one of the easiest slimes you will ever make. You'll need:

- Scissors
- Empty plastic bottle
- Measuring cup
- Cornstarch

- Balloons

- Water

Take three tablespoons of cornstarch and mix it with some water until the mixture starts to feel slimy. You should be able to pick it up and model things about of it. Of course, you will get dirty hands doing so!

Next you pour the slime or place the slime into an empty bottle. Follow this by putting your balloon over the bottle opening, as though the bottle was a balloon pump.

You can then slowly slide your slime into the balloon. Your balloon will fill and then you will need to squeeze on the bottle to stretch the walls of the balloon and ensure it is packed full.

Once it is the right size simply and carefully remove the bottle and tie off the balloon. It is a good idea to snip of the excess without damaging your knot.

You should then get a second balloon, cut the end of it off and glide it over the first one. Again it will need to be tied off. This will make your stress ball stronger and it less likely that you have slime exploding everywhere!

Then all you need to do is start using it!

2. Glue Ball

This option uses glue to create a slime ball that can be held in a pot and squished with your fingers, much like you can buy in the shops as children's toys.

You will need:

- Food coloring
- Liquid starch
- Clear Elmer's glue
- Water
- Mixing bowl & spoon
- Measuring cup

To create your new slime ball pour some glue into a mixing bowl and add a few drops of food coloring; this will make your slime ball a unique color.

Next add a little water and half a cup of starch liquid. This should be done slowly, mixing as you go. You can adjust the amount of water to create the right consistency; this is personal preference not a set consistency.

Once you have finished mixing it is best to pour the slime into a pot and leave it for a couple of hours. This will allow the slime to half set and feel smooth when you stick your fingers into it later.

You don't need to keep it in the pot when de-stressing, the pot provides a convenient means of storing your new creation. The great thing about this slime is that it will fill any size or shape container. It is also very smooth to the touch.

3. Glitter Slime

This is a variant on the glue ball as it uses a very similar recipe but provides nice, glittering stress relieving slime.

You will need:

- Water
- Liquid starch

- Glitter glue
- Acrylic Paint

Of course you still need a mixing bowl and spoon! Again you will need to add some glitter glue into a bowl; the exact quantity will depend upon how large you wish your slime to be. Then add a touch of acrylic paint; the color choice is all yours. This will help to bind the ingredient together and add some color to the slime. You can then add half a cup of liquid starch; stir it in slowly. This is followed by a little water; make sure you add just a little at a time until you find the right consistency.

Again, this can now be put into the pot and left for a couple of hours before you start using it.

4. Lavender Putty

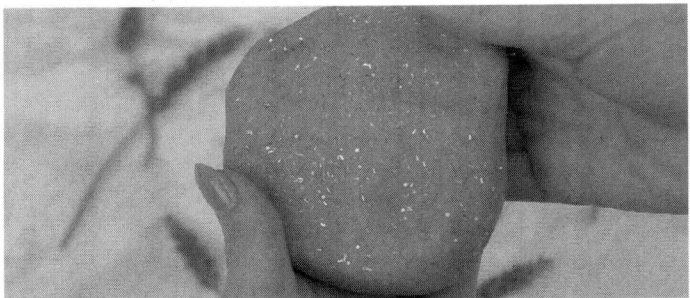

This is just like holding a ball of putty but without the stickiness. The addition of lavender will help you to unwind; its scent is naturally calming. Research actually shows it will reduce your heart rate and help you to simply chill, no matter what is going on round you.

You will need:

- Cup of boiling water
- Cup of salt
- 2 cups flour
- 6 tablespoons cream of tartar
- 2 tablespoons of a carrier oil, such as almond or coconut. They must complement the smell of lavender.
- 30 drops lavender oil
- Food coloring

To create the ultimate de-stressing putty, start by mixing all the flour with the salt. Then add the cream of tartar, carrier oil and the lavender oil before slowly adding the boiling water, stirring as you do so.

It should almost immediately become putty like. It is important to add the boiling water slowly to ensure the mixture doesn't become too liquid.

If you want you can now add a few drops of food coloring, the choice of color is entirely yours. You can then add extra flour if the putty is too sticky.

The mixture will take approximately 30 minutes to cool before you can start manipulating it; have fun de-stressing!

5. Scented Goo

The above recipe uses the power of lavender as a calming mechanism but you can choose virtually any aroma. Providing you like the scent it will help to calm you and lower your stress levels. This works by triggering the release of endorphins, simply because you are feeling happier!

This option adds a scent in to your goo, the range of aromas is virtually limitless.

You will need:

- Glue, any sort of liquid glue will do.
- Mixing bowl and spoon
- Measuring jug

- Essential oil; your choice of aroma.
- Food coloring
- Borax crystals

Start by putting approximately 4 ounces of glue into a bowl and then mix in approximately 3 ounces of warm water; not boiling.

Once you have stirred this thoroughly you can add four or five drop of food coloring. The color is up to you, the more coloring you add the darker it will be. You can even leave the coloring out if you want it to be white.

Next add 3 or 4 drops of your chosen aromatic oil and stir until it is all blended.

Separately you need to put quarter of a cup of boiling water into a measuring jug with 2/3 teaspoon of borax crystals. They should dissolve fully before you pour it into your glue mixture.

This will absorb quickly into the glue mixture and it is important you keep stirring the whole time. As soon as it has become slime like you need to continue kneading it with your hands. This will ensure the mixture is blended properly and there are no lumps.

That's it; you're ready to start de-stressing!

6. The Squidgy Slime Ball

This variant of the slime ball is designed to be placed inside a net. This will allow you to squeeze it and watch it pop out of all the holes, before it disappears back inside. It can literally give you hours of fun for virtually no cost.

You will need:

- Bottle of liquid glue
- Liquid starch
- 2 cups of water.

Start by pouring the whole bottle of liquid glue into a bowl. This should be 4 fluid ounces. Then put a little water in the glue bottle and swish it round before adding it to the glue.

Mix thoroughly then add a tablespoon of liquid starch. The mixture will immediately start to become gooey. Add a little more until you get a slime like putty that you can pick up in your hands and stretch without getting sticky.

You will then need to put the mixture into a bottle and pour it into a colorful balloon by covering the end of the bottle with the balloon. A striped balloon adds a nice effect but it can be any style you like.

Next you need to get a piece of betting, like the ones you get round fruit. Cut a piece big enough to wrap round your putty filled balloon and encase it in the netting. Tie this off and your stress ball is ready.

The harder you squeeze the more it will come out of the netting holes, making it fun as well as de-stressing.

7. Slime Without Liquid starch (Shampoo)

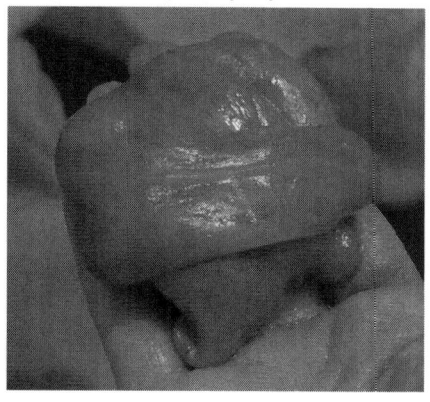

It is possible that the borax found in liquid starch that is used in many DIY slime balls could burn your fingers, although there have not yet been any reported cases of it.

To avoid the risk it is best to avoid using liquid starch. This recipe will create a 'fluffy' de-stress slime.

You will need:

- ½ cup shampoo
- ¼ cup cornstarch
- Food coloring
- Water
- Mixing bowl

Start by mixing the shampoo and cornstarch together in one bowl. You can then add several drops of food coloring to get the color of your choice.

Next add 6 tablespoons of water and stir as you add each spoonful. You should have a dough like mixture that you can knead with your hands. You may need to knead it for several minutes.

If needed you can always add extra cornstarch to create the right consistency; this will need to be a personal decision.

That's it, your fluffy slime is ready to use.

8. Volcano Fluffy Slime

This has the same fluffy texture as the previous mix but it has an extra component. If you add heat it will melt and then, as it cools become fluffy again; much like lava!

You will need:

- ¼ cup liquid glue

- ½ cup cornstarch

- Food coloring

- Mixing bowl

Start by mixing the glue and the cornstarch until blended smooth. You can then add a few drops of food coloring to get your desired color.

You will need to mix thoroughly before kneading it for at least ten minutes!

You can then heat it in the microwave for 20 seconds before kneading it for a further 10 minutes. Then start feeling the stress leaving your body as you play with lava!

9. Sand Slime

Without borax this mixture will not be as smooth, hence the title sand slime. However, it will be as stretchy and gooey!

You will need:

- 1 cup liquid glue
- 1 tablespoon baking soda
- 1 tablespoon contact lens solution
- Food coloring

To start mix your glue and baking soda together until you have a smooth blend. You can then add any food coloring you want to get your choice of color.

Once this is mixed add your contact lens solution and mix for several minutes. If necessary add a little more contact lens solution until you reach the right consistency.

It is worth noting that if the consistency is soggy then kneading it can resolve this. As soon as you have the right consistency you can use it or find a suitable place to store it.

10. **Magnetic Slime**

This is good for de-stressing but also a lot of fun for any child:

You will need:

- Liquid starch
- Liquid glue
- Iron Oxide powder
- Neodymium magnet

- Mixing bowl

Start by putting ½ cup of the liquid starch in your mixing bowl and adding 4 tablespoons of the Iron oxide powder. You will need to blend it thoroughly.

Next add ½ cup liquid glue and stir! This will take several minutes to look like anything other than a mess. Once mixed you will be able to remove the slime and knead it with your hands, (which will get black).

You can then pat the slime with some paper towel until the excess liquid has been removed. As soon as it is dry you can start to use it. As well as de-stressing by kneading it you will be able to wave your neodymium magnet over it and make it move without touching it!

11. Saline Slime

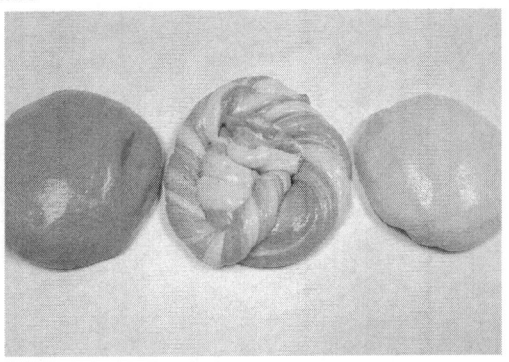

This is just another way of making your standard slime.

You will need:

- ½ cup liquid glue

- 1 Tablespoon saline solution

- ½ cup water

- ½ teaspoon baking soda

- Food coloring

- The usual tools

Start by combining your liquid glue with your water and stirring thoroughly. You can then add a dozen drops of food coloring and even some glitter to create your desired effect.

Again, stir the mixture thoroughly.

You then need to add the baking soda and stir which will dry the mixture out a little. Then add the saline solution and stir quickly. The chemical reaction will be quick and you need to have it all mixed together

As soon as it looks like you can easily remove it from your bowl you need to use your hands to knead the mixture for approximately 5 minutes.

That's it, you can play straight away.

12. Crunchy Slime

This adds a nice touch to the slime de-stressing tool as you can feel the crunch every time you squeeze the slime.

You will need:

- Liquid glue
- Food coloring
- Water
- Baking soda
- Saline solution
- Beads
- Mixing implements

Start by mixing ½ cup of liquid glue with the same amount of water. You can then color your slime, if you want to. If you've used transparent glue it can look goo without the food coloring.

You can then add ½ teaspoon of baking soda, followed by half a cup of small beads. Don't put too any beads in as this will affect the stretchiness. Less is definitely more!

You are now ready to add a tablespoon of saline solution and mix fast! If necessary add a little extra saline solution. Your slime will then be ready to knead. The beads make an unusual sensation in your hands, helping to distract and de-stress you.

13. Floam Slime

This is effectively the same recipe as the one above. However, instead of adding beads you can add foam balls; obviously very small ones! This will give the slime a squishy ball type texture which will feel particularly funny in your hand!

14. Super Stretchy Slime

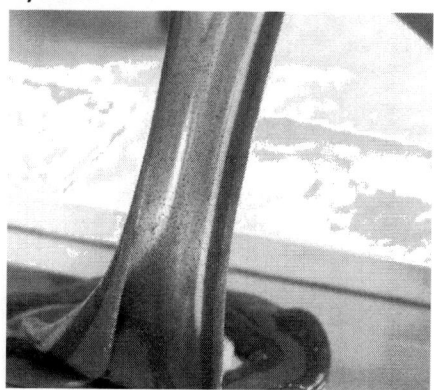

Slime is supposed to be stretchy but this recipe takes it a step further and makes it super stretchy!

You will need:

- Standard eye drops
- Liquid glue
- Baking soda
- Food coloring

½ cu of liquid glue needs to be placed into your mixing bowl and then add 6 drops of food coloring, or as much as you need to get the desired effect. You can then mix in a teaspoon of baking powder and mix thoroughly.

You now need to add forty to fifty eye drops but you should do this ten at a time to ensure you get the consistency right. When it is still slightly sticky put a few eye drops on your hands and lift the mixture out of the bowl. You can then knead it for several minutes until it's no longer sticky to the touch.

Keep it in a container and use whenever you want!

15. Putty Slime

This is another version of the putty mentioned earlier and an effective stress reliever which can be easily carried with you.

You will need:

- Water
- Liquid glue
- Borax powder

- Food coloring

Again you need to start with ¼ glue and add a few drops of food coloring to get your desired color. Separately you need to mix ¼ teaspoon of borax powder with the same amount of warm water. This can then be added to the glue mix, stir as you add it will react quickly.

After a few minutes continue the mixing process by hand; you don't even need to wait for it to cool to start using it.

16. Edible Slime!

It is possible to de-stress and carry a snack with you, although I can't guarantee it will be tasty!

You will need:

- 3 packs Gelatin
- Water
- Food coloring
- Corn syrup

Follow the instructions on the gelatin packs to make the gelatin; this should just require boiling water. Once this has been done you need to add ¼ cup of corn syrup and blend it thoroughly. To finish add a little color; any one is fine!

More corn syrup will allow you to stretch the slime more. However, you should be aware that this is sticky slime and not for everyone!

17. Soap Slime

This slime is actually the product of two processes, exploding soap followed by slime!

Start by putting a bar of soap in a big glass dish and then putting it into the microwave for two minutes. It will explode into a huge ball of foam. This can then be chopped into small pieces.

Simply add a little water and mix thoroughly. Too much and you will have a liquid slime so take this part slowly.

Once it reaches the right consistency you're good to start playing!

18. Two Ingredient Slime

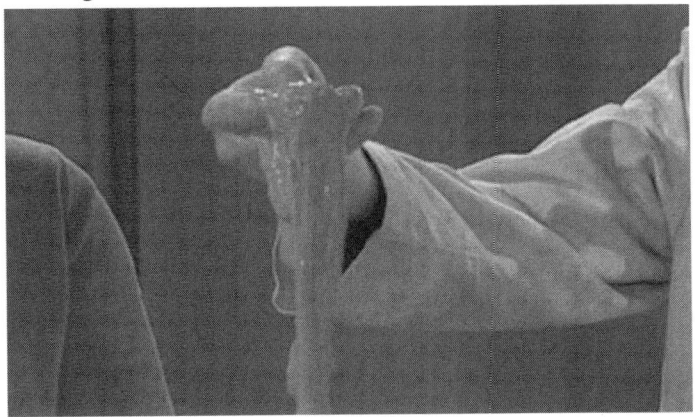

Did you know that you could make slime with just two ingredients with a third as an optional extra? Here's how.

You will need:

- Cornstarch
- Liquid glue
- Optional food coloring

Put some glue in a mixing bowl and add a few drops of food coloring. Then simply add three times as much cornstarch as the amount of glue you used.

You need to add the starch slowly, stirring all the time until the mixture thickens. Once it stops being sticky to the touch you can continue to knead it with your hands. A few minutes of kneading will suffice to finish preparing your stress relieving slime.

19. No Glue Slime – Chia Seed

This is a different approach which produces a slightly sticky version of the slime but it is a lot of fun!

You will need:

- Chia Seeds
- Water
- Cornstarch
- Food coloring

You need to put two cups of water with ¼ cup if chia seeds in a container and leave them to soak overnight; preferably in the fridge.

The following day you can stir the seeds to break up any clumps and add a teaspoon of xanthan gum along with a few drops of your preferred food coloring.

Once you've mixed this gently you can add 16 ounces of cornstarch and keep mixing. As soon as it is too hard to mix with a spoon you can knead it with your hands. You may need a little extra cornstarch to get rid of the sticky feel.

It should be noted that this is made with food products so it will perish over time.

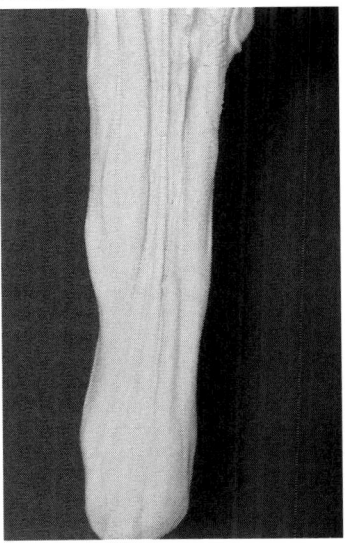

20. Seedless No Glue Slime

Seeds create the stretch in your slime without them you may find your slime is more brittle but can still be a good stress reliever.

You will need:

- Water
- Xanthan gum
- Food coloring
- Cornstarch

Simply mix 2 cups of water with 1 ¼ tablespoons of xanthan gum. Then add a little food coloring followed by 16 ounces of cornstarch.

Again mix until you can no longer do so with the spoon and then start kneading it by hand. Adding cornstarch reduces stickiness while extra water can stop crumbling problems.

Chapter 2 – 10 Fun Variations OF Slime Recipes

There are so any potentially good recipes for slime that it is hard to choose the best 30. But, the ones in this book are all very easy to make and satisfying.

Here are 10 variations which can be just as fun and help to relieve your stress.

1. No Borax Slime
You will need:

- Body wash
- Food coloring
- Water Cornstarch

Start with two tablespoons of body wash in a bowl and add a few drops of food coloring until you have a uniform color of your choice. Then simply add approximately the same amount of cornstarch to your bowl and keep mixing.

You will need to knead it with your hands to finish the process. A little water can make your slime stretchier.

2. Liquid Soap Glitter Slime

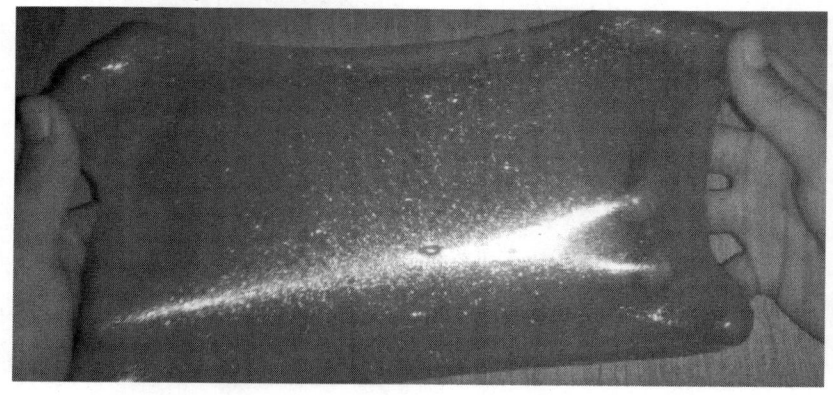

You will need:

- Cornstarch
- Food coloring
- Dish soap
- Glitter

This is a really quick way to make slime. Simply add four tablespoons of liquid hand soap to a bowl and mix in as much food coloring as you need to make your desired color. Add in plenty of glitter to the mix.

Then add approximately the same amount of cornstarch and mix. Within 10 -20 seconds you will struggle to mix it with your spoon. This is your cue to remove it by hand and knead it.

After a few minutes of kneading you will have slime and relieved you stress in the making process!

3. Yoghurt Slime!

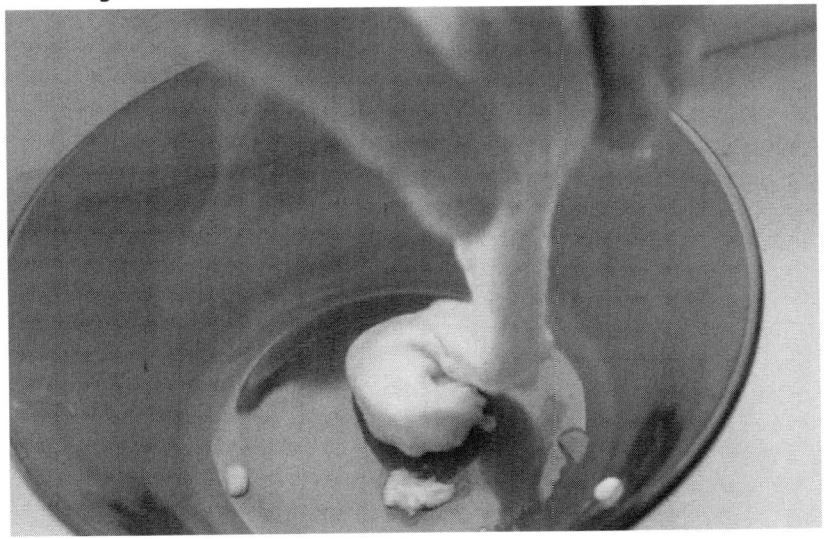

This actually works even though you might not think it would!

You will need:

- Yogurt – plain
- Cornstarch
- Coloring

Mix the same amount of cornstarch with yoghurt to form a stiff mixture. Add a few drops of coloring and then keep mixing before switching to kneading.

After approximately ten minutes of kneading you'll have slime!

Of course this is edible so will not last that long!

4. Borax & Glue Free Slime

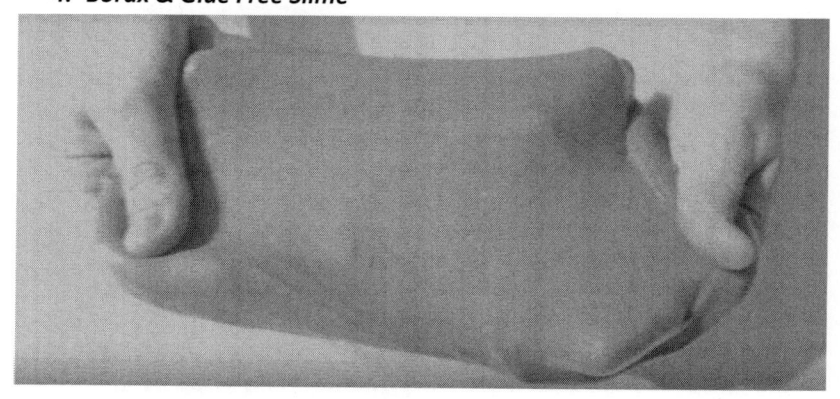

You will need:

- Liquid glue, preferably clear although white can be used.
- Laundry detergent – in powder form
- Water

Start by putting 4 ounces of glue into a mixing bowl. Then add two tablespoons of laundry detergent powder. This must be done slowly to allow you to mix it thoroughly. Keep mixing as you add a tablespoon or two of water.

Once it has all blended and clumped together you can knead it with your hands, after several minutes the slime will start to form!

5. Rainbow Slime

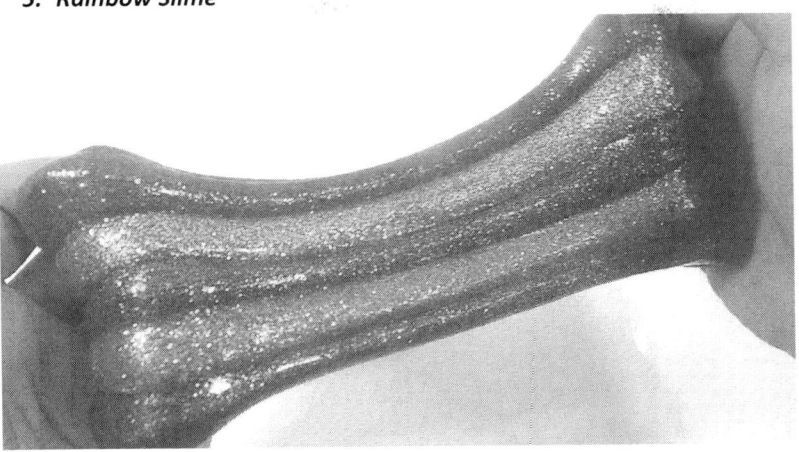

You will need:

- Glitter glue – 4 tubes each of a different color
- 1 teaspoon borax
- 2 tablespoons water

Start by emptying each of your glitter tubes into their own bowls. Then mix your borax and water thoroughly. Add a little borax to the first color and stir until it lifts away from the side of the bowl. Then knead it by hand until it is soft, not sticky.

You will then need to repeat this process with the other color glitter glues.

Roughly roll each piece of slime so that you have four sausages against each other. All you need to do then is pinch the sausages together and start stretching from the ends. The colors will stretch and become rainbow slime!

6. Heated Slime

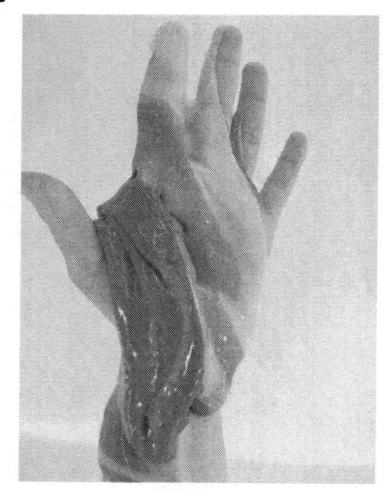

You will need:

- Liquid glue – ¼ cup
- Thermochromic pigment – 3 teaspoons
- Water – 1 tablespoon
- Liquid starch – ¼ cup
- Food coloring

Put your liquid glue in the mixing bowl and add the water and 5 drops of your preferred food coloring. Once mixed add the thermochromic pigment and stir again.

Add the liquid starch and you will have a slimy mixture which can be kneaded with your hands. One ready you can use it or store it.

The slime will change color in the sunlight thanks to the warmth and the thermochromic pigments!

7. Glow in the Dark

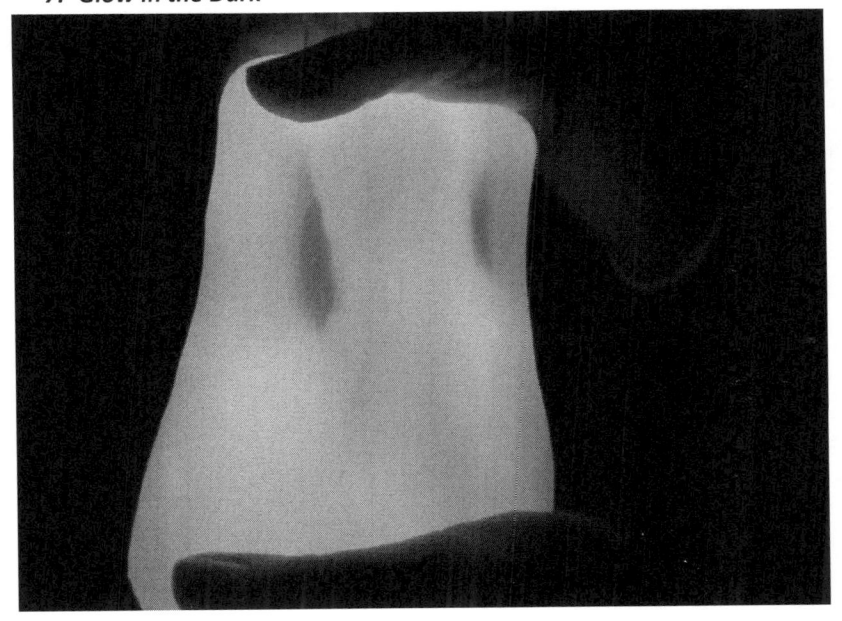

This is just fun!

You will need:

- Liquid starch
- Liquid glue

- Glow in the dark paint

Place ½ cup of liquid starch in a bowl and add 3 tablespoons of glow in the dark pint. Once mixed properly you can add ½ cup of liquid glue.

Stir thoroughly then place on a paper towel to absorb excess water. You can then knead it with your hands; it will slowly go from messy to slimy and will glow in the dark!

8. Confetti Slime

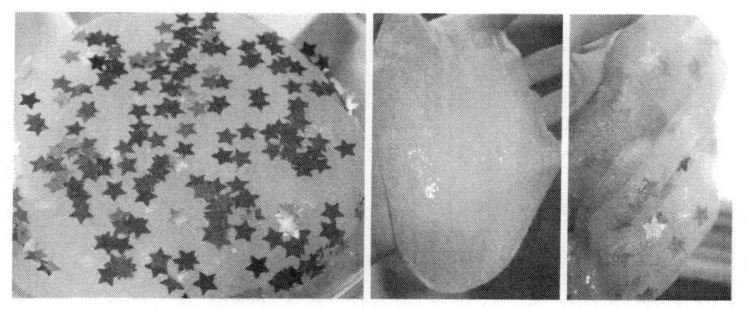

You will need:

- Water
- Liquid starch
- Confetti
- Liquid glue

Mix 4 ounces of liquid glue with 2 tablespoons of liquid starch and one tablespoon of water. Add in your confetti and mix thoroughly.

When it is mixed you will need to put it onto a paper towel to remove excess liquid and then knead it until it becomes very attractive slime!

9. Bubbling Slime

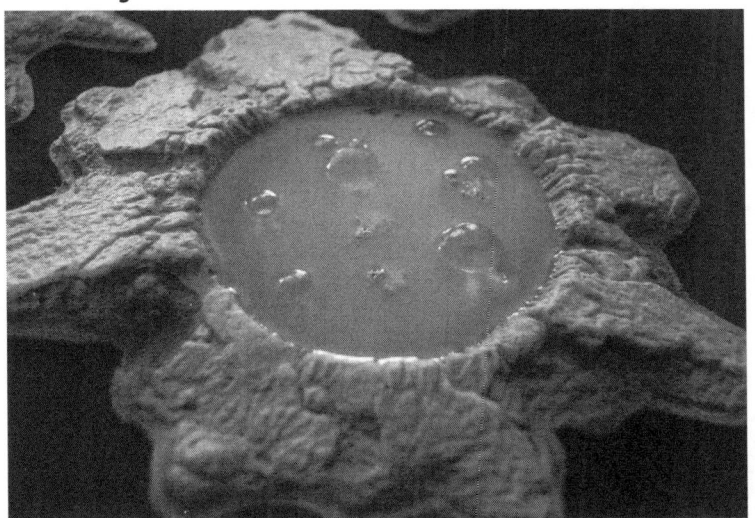

This slime actually bubbles and continues to do so for hours after you have made it.

You will need:

- Xanthan gum
- White vinegar
- Baking soda
- Food coloring

Start by putting 2 cup of white vinegar in a bowl and whisking whole adding the xanthan gum. You can also add any food coloring you fancy. As you will struggle to get rid of all the xanthan gum it is best to put the mixture in the fridge for several hours; this will dissolve them.

Once removed you can whisk it again to make it creamy and very gooey.

Now cover the bottom of your storage tub with baking soda and pour your slime mixture over it. It will bubble for hours and the bubbles will become trapped in your slime. Alternatively you can mix the baking soda in to get the trapped bubbles look but not see them bubbling.

10. The Most Basic Slime

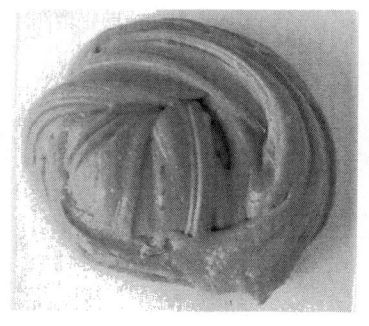

This is for when you are in a hurry.

All you need it 2 cups of cornstarch, one of water and a few drops of food coloring. Mix and then keep mixing. It will eventually become slime!

To speed this process up you can actually warm it slightly; this will speed the chemical reaction between these two substances.

Conclusion

No matter which way you look at it slime is fun! Making it is generally very easy and you only need a few simple household ingredients. You can make it with your children to bond and tech them a little about chemistry.

More importantly you can take most of these slimes with you, either in a container or in your pocket. This will allow you to squeeze; poke or prod the slime as hard as possible when you are in a stressful situation.

You will feel less stressed as you are distracted and the pleasure of poking or pulling slime is contagious even as an adult. Even if you have it on your desk at work you will find others recognize its value and may even ask you how you have managed to make it yourself.

There are many ways to de-stress. One of the easiest is to remove yourself from a stressful situation but this is not always possible or a good idea. Your stress relieving slime is acceptable in almost any situation and will make you feel better.

Perhaps the best thing is that, with the aid of this book, you can easily replace any slime which has been lost or damaged. You can also try a wide variety of different types of slime and experiment with your own recipes; there is really no limit to what is possible!